100HI-TECH**PENTATONIC** GUITARLICKS

Discover the Language of Advanced Technical Rock Guitar Soloing

IOANNIS**ANASTASSAKIS**

FUNDAMENTAL**CHANGES**

100 Hi-Tech Pentatonic Guitar Licks

Discover the Language of Advanced Technical Rock Guitar Soloing

Published by **www.fundamental-changes.com**

ISBN: 978-1-78933-394-7

For over 350 Free Guitar Lessons with Videos Check Out

www.fundamental-changes.com

Join our Facebook Community of cool musicians

www.facebook.com/groups/fundamentalguitar

Instagram: **FundamentalChanges**

Cover Image Copyright: Shutterstock, pixfly

Contents

Introduction

Music is a language, and mastering any language includes learning a significant amount of vocabulary. The pentatonic scale is one of the basic building blocks, and an important part, of the language of the electric guitar. Countless songs that have inspired millions to pick up the instrument contain pentatonic melodies.

To successfully bring the sound of the pentatonic scale into the 21st Century, we need to modernize our approach to using it, and take it beyond standard blues phrases and '70s classic rock clichés. One way to achieve this is by learning phrases that combine the pentatonic scale with contemporary, hi-tech guitar techniques, to make it sound fresh, modern and relevant.

Arpeggios, melodic sequencing, wide intervals, pedal points, and multi-octave triads have all been available to pianists, saxophonists and violinists for years, but were rarely used in rock guitar until the '70s, due to the inherent difficulties of performing them on the instrument. But guitar technique has moved on and today we have many more possibilities.

The pentatonic scale is made up of five notes, so it sits right in between diatonic scales (seven notes) and triads/arpeggios (three and four notes) in terms of its complexity. It has been the cornerstone of electric blues/ rock guitar for a long time, so combining it with hi-tech techniques is an instant way to sound modern without using unusual scales or compromising the rock-like quality of your playing

This book offers the intermediate to advanced electric guitarist an exciting collection of musical phrases that use the pentatonic scale in progressively more original ways. Use this book like a buffet; pick and choose the phrases and licks that appeal to you the most. Not all the licks will appeal to everyone, so audition them by listening to the audio tracks, and start by learning the ones you like best.

If you feel any pain in your hands, fingers or wrist when practising these licks, especially the ones with wide stretches, stop playing immediately. Take a break and try again later, taking things slowly, when your hand and fingers have recovered. If you continue to experience pain while you play, you should see a specialist.

If you're ready to dive in, check out the audio for Chapter One and let's get going!

Get the Audio

The audio files for this book are available to download for free from **www.fundamental-changes.com.** The link is in the top right-hand corner. Simply select this book title from the drop-down menu and follow the instructions to get the audio.

We recommend that you download the files directly to your computer, not to your tablet, and extract them there before adding them to your media library. You can then put them on your tablet, iPod or burn them to a CD. On the download page, there is a help PDF and we also provide technical support via the contact form.

For over 350 Free Guitar Lessons with Videos Check Out

www.fundamental-changes.com

Join our Facebook Community of cool musicians

www.facebook.com/groups/fundamentalguitar

Instagram: **FundamentalChanges**

Chapter One: Legato

Let's begin our journey into hi-tech pentatonic licks by exploring *legato* (using hammer-ons and pull-offs to achieve smooth, horn-like articulation). It is probably the most widely used technique in this book. We can find legato licks in all levels and styles of guitar playing, such as jazz, country, blues, and rock.

Many of the licks we'll examine in later chapters use legato as an integral part of their technical execution, so it's important to work through this section before tackling them.

When playing legato, it's important to be aware of your playing dynamics and use them deliberately. This means controlling whether there is a pronounced difference in the dynamic of picked notes and hammered notes, or whether they have the same attack.

Our first example is a classic rock E Minor Pentatonic lick, which combines legato with a quick sweep between the first and the second strings. Similar patterns can be found in the playing of Gary Moore, John Sykes and Doug Aldrich. Pick the first note on each string with a down stroke and use hammer-ons and pull-offs for the rest.

This is a nice lick that sounds great in isolation, but we will use it as a springboard to play several extended ideas in subsequent examples.

To stop unwanted string noise, position the tip of your first finger to touch and slightly mute the second string.

Example 1a:

The next E Minor idea is an expansion of Example 1a that adds more repetitions and expands the finger stretch on the first string.

The mechanics are the same, meaning you only need to use one downstroke on each string, then use hammer-ons and pull-offs for the rest of the notes. We find several examples like this in the playing of John Sykes, Gary Moore, Zakk Wylde and other contemporary hard-rock players.

Stop and rest your hands if you feel any discomfort when playing the 12th fret to 17th stretch on the first string.

Example 1b:

This next E Minor lick requires a bit more of a stretch in the fretting hand.

It is based on an extended pentatonic pattern popularized by Kee Marcello (Europe) and is an excellent way to create a sequence of 1/16th notes using two adjacent minor pentatonic shapes.

Follow the fingering closely.

Example 1c:

Here's a Paul Gilbert style A Minor Pentatonic sextuplet sequence that uses fast, precise legato to create a repeating twelve-note pattern.

Take some time to memorize this line carefully and practice it slowly with a metronome. Make sure you use the specific picking outlined here, because you will need to use it for more elaborate phrases that appear later in the book.

Example 1d:

This next phrase is a combination of several ascending and descending E Minor Pentatonic triplet shapes that connect to create a long, flowing melody. This is one of my favourite legato pentatonic licks and similar to phrases you can hear in the playing of Joe Bonamassa and Gary Moore.

I have outlined my preferred picking pattern, which is optimized for speed, but you can use whatever works for you. Use light pick strokes and aim for a fluid execution.

Example 1e:

This next Paul Gilbert style A Minor phrase is a variation of Example 1e, which is expanded to use all six strings of the guitar.

The phrase is played in strict 1/16th notes, which can be a challenge due to the combination of string crossing and legato. Memorize the picking directions as below, even though they might seem counterintuitive to begin with.

You don't have to play the whole lick when soloing, so feel free to mix and match the parts that sound most interesting to you.

Example 1f:

It's always a good idea to explore rhythmic variations of your licks to help you improvise at different speeds and in different styles. This lick is another elaboration of the previous idea. It adds two more notes and also changes the rhythm to 1/16th note triplets.

Once again, pay attention to the written picking directions and try not to deviate from them.

Example 1g:

This A Minor phrase is a straightforward legato pattern that repeats in ascending octaves to create a long, fluid line that avoids sounding traditionally pentatonic. Don't worry too much about the fact that the pattern is 13 notes long – just practice it as regular 1/16th notes when memorizing it.

After you have memorized the first 13 notes, the fingering pattern remains the same and repeats one octave higher.

The most challenging part of the lick is moving between the first and second finger on the 3rd fret. This will take some getting used to if you are not well-versed in wide stretches. Keep your fretting hand straight and the thumb behind the neck.

Example 1h:

This fun A Minor lick is our introduction to rhythmic displacement.

It is a five-note descending pattern played as straight 1/16th notes, to create an extremely interesting cross rhythmic effect, as a different note falls on the downbeats in each beat.

This should not be a difficult lick to master provided you are comfortable with pull-offs. The main challenge is playing a five-note pattern in strict 1/16th notes. Practicing with a slow metronome when memorizing the lick will help a lot.

Example 1i:

This A Minor lick is particularly fun to play. It combines three different pentatonic sequences – a three-note, a five-note, and a four-note sequence – to create a longer twelve-note sequence that is played on the top three strings in 1/16th notes.

The sequence is repeated on other three-string sets to create an exciting angular effect.

Example 1j:

This line uses a combination of legato, a mini-sweep, and a moderately wide stretch to create a fluid, repeating A Minor phrase that adds an interesting twist to the standard pentatonic sound. You can hear similar phrases in the playing of George Lynch of *Dokken*.

Use a light pick attack. The sound of the pick should be almost imperceptible in order for it to blend well with all the hammer-ons and pull-offs, and make sure you follow the fingering directions.

Example 1k:

To finish this chapter here's another expansion of Example 1a, but this time we'll add an E Blues scale note. The mechanics of the phrase remain the same, but a little more finger agility is required to play the stretch on the first string. Similar patterns can be found in the playing of Gary Moore, George Lynch, John Sykes and Doug Aldrich.

The combination of legato and a quick two-string sweep between the first and second strings will need some work to get the timing correct.

Example 1l:

Chapter Two: Sweeping

Sweeping is an extremely useful guitar technique and was popularized in the mid-1980s by several guitar virtuosos, most notably the fusion legend, Frank Gambale.

The basic idea of sweeping is fairly simple: when you need to change strings, move the pick in the direction of the string you are moving towards.

If you are moving from a higher to lower string, always use an upstroke.

If you are moving from a lower to a higher string, always use a downstroke.

This way, instead of using alternate picking to play adjacent strings, you use one long sweeping motion to play multiple strings with a single movement, kind of like a broken strum.

Let's explore sweeping in a pentatonic context by examining this variation of a John Petrucci lick. The pattern reworks the usual two-notes-per-string shape of E Minor Pentatonic, to one that uses three notes on the first string and one note on the second string to create a three-string sweep shape.

Even though all the notes are pentatonic, the combination of legato and sweeping changes the timbre significantly and renders the scale quite difficult to recognize. Follow the picking directions closely and take care to minimize string noise when changing strings. The best way to achieve good muting is to use the tip of each fretting finger to slightly touch and mute the string immediately below it.

I find it easier to angle the pick slightly in the direction I am travelling, as this reduces the resistance when string crossing.

Example 2a:

This next example uses a pattern made popular by Kee Marcello. The shape is a combination of two adjacent E Minor Pentatonic shapes and is played in quintuplets. It's a fluid lick that sounds impressive when played fast.

Memorize the picking directions and use sweeps when changing strings.

Once you have memorized the pattern on the second and first strings, things become much easier, since it is repeated diatonically on the next two-string sets. The biggest challenge is playing the mini-sweeps in strict quintuplets, because most players tend to rush them. Practice to gain control over the phrasing.

Example 2b:

The following A Minor phrase is based on shapes used by Frank Gambale. In this example, I superimpose arpeggios that are diatonic to the minor pentatonic scale as I descend across the three-string sets.

Pay attention to the picking directions and do not change them. The use of a rolling barre with the first finger on the 5th fret might be a little challenging to perform cleanly, as the muting is fairly difficult.

The best way to learn this and play it cleanly is to start slow and concentrate on the string change with the first finger. I often have my students isolate the motion of the string change and repeat it over and over until they can play it with a clean technique.

Example 2c:

This next A Minor idea is one of my favourite pentatonic sweeping licks and reminds me of something a fusion saxophone player might play. The picking patterns are optimized to take full advantage of sweeping, by arranging the notes of the A Minor Pentatonic scale in a way that facilitates sweeps across the strings.

This lick will test your ability to combine alternate picking with sweeping, since the techniques switch several times. Once again, the phrasing of the lick masks the obvious minor pentatonic sound.

Keep your thumb behind (not on top of) the neck to help you shift between the different positions smoothly.

Example 2d:

This next A Minor lick expands on the pattern in Example 2c.

It uses 1/16th notes and emphasizes the vertical movement to create phrases that extend from the first to the sixth string via a combination of minor 7 and suspended arpeggios.

To avoid unwanted string noise, roll your first finger as you play adjacent notes on consecutive strings. To practice this idea, isolate the notes played by the first finger on the 5th fret until you can produce a clean sound when changing strings.

Example 2e:

Here's another Frank Gambale style phrase. We stick to the top three strings, but ascend the neck using identical Sus2 arpeggio shapes that are contained in the A Minor Pentatonic scale. Follow the picking directions closely.

Keep your thumb behind, not on top of the neck, to help you shift between positions smoothly.

Frank often plays a variation of this lick, where he plays each position twice, instead of just once. This makes the lick easier, since you have more time to prepare for the position shifts.

Example 2f:

This next E Minor phrase uses a fairly unorthodox shape for E Minor Pentatonic. There are three notes on the first string, one note on the second, and three on the third string.

This is done to facilitate the use of sweeping, by keeping an odd number of notes on each string. Take care to avoid string noise, especially when moving from the second to third string.

Example 2g:

Here's one of my favourite pentatonic sweeping licks where the combination of hammer-ons, slides, and sweeps creates a fluid approach.

This phrase uses several inversions of both the Am7 arpeggio and the A Minor Pentatonic scale.

It's easy to rush the slides or the legato parts, so practice this with a metronome. It can be a challenge to keep the rhythm as you switch between different techniques and positions.

Example 2h:

The following A Minor Pentatonic lick is an elaboration of Example 2h, which combines playing concepts popularized by Frank Gambale and Richie Kotzen. Each position is a different three-string inversion of an Am7 arpeggio, seamlessly connected to create a longer melodic phrase.

Make sure you use your third finger on the 7th fret to help shift into the next position smoothly.

Example 2i:

The following phrase is based on an idea by metal monster guitarist Rusty Cooley and uses four A Minor Pentatonic scale notes to outline an Am7 arpeggio across three strings.

Even though the shape is simple it can be tricky to synchronize the left and right hands, but once that is in place it becomes easy to speed up. Muting unwanted string noise is also a challenge here – make sure you slightly lift each finger after a note has sounded – you definitely want to avoid one note bleeding into the next, especially if you're play with distortion.

Use the second finger of the fretting as an anchor point as it remains at the 13th fret throughout. This stable point of reference helps you change between the two arpeggio shapes.

Example 2j:

This A Minor lick is a good test of your sliding and position shifting skills.

Based on two different positions of the Am7 arpeggio, it uses a repeating picking pattern to help string crossing, and the quintuplets make it rhythmically unique. Follow the picking directions closely; they are optimized for maximum speed and efficiency. All position shifts are performed with the fourth finger on the first string, and the first finger on the third string.

Example 2k:

The following phrase uses sweep picking to move through various inversions of the Am7 arpeggio. It is important to follow the picking directions to the letter, otherwise you'll never be able to speed it up.

This 1/16th notes phrase is played in five-note shapes to create an exciting cross-rhythmic effect. Use your third finger on the 13th fret to help you shift into the next position smoothly.

Example 2l:

The following A Minor lick is probably one of the most impressive in the whole book when played at a fast tempo.

It is not a difficult phrase to memorize, since it uses an identical shape that moves up the neck, but keeping the left and right hands synchronized will probably prove challenging for most players.

It's definitely a lick worth learning and adding to your arsenal of hi-tech pentatonic approaches.

Example 2m:

Here's another of my favourite A Minor sweeping licks, which creates a fluid, saxophone-style effect. Make sure you angle the pick in the direction you are sweeping.

Example 2n:

The final E Minor Pentatonic sweeping lick of this chapter is based on the playing of Eric Johnson and highlights a distinctive playing mechanic often used to facilitate smooth string crossing.

Typical of Johnson, this line contains a lot of rhythm displacement, where five-note melodies are played in 1/16th note rhythms, so that the strong notes of the phrase keep falling on different beat divisions. Take care to not miss any of the sweeps that consistently occur between the last note of one pattern and the first note of the next.

Example 2o:

I hope you enjoyed these unusual sweeping ideas and found a few interesting concepts to help spice up your pentatonic playing.

Let's move on and learn to add tapping to our pentatonic ideas.

Chapter Three: Tapping

Tapping was popularized by Eddie Van Halen in the late 1970s and quickly became one of his trademark techniques. Even though he did not invent tapping, he was responsible for making it a part of the modern guitarist's repertoire.

So, what's the appeal of tapping?

- It makes it easier to play much larger intervals on the guitar at high speed

- It creates a fluid dynamic, since one string can be used for several notes without picking

- It's easier to play faster, since you can use both hands to produce notes. This way the workload is split between the left and right hands

These minor pentatonic tapping phrases will probably become a prized addition to your vocabulary. They are not presented in order of difficulty, so feel free to mix and match the ones that get your heart racing.

The first phrase is based on the A Minor Pentatonic box. It is one of the easiest licks to play, but still sounds great. Taps only occur on the 12th and 14th frets, which makes it easy to keep track of their position. The fretting hand pattern is also the same on both strings.

Follow the fingering directions and hold the pick between the thumb and first finger while tapping with the middle finger.

Example 3a:

This impressive E Minor lick combines tapping with a moderately wide stretch to play four pentatonic notes on a single string.

Practice with a metronome, as it's easy for rhythmic inconsistencies to creep in.

Example 3b:

This is a great little E Minor lick that's heavily influenced by the maestro Steve Vai, and is based on playing sextuplets with a twist. The fourth note of the pattern is the same pitch as the third, and is played on the same string and fret, but is played with the tapping finger on the repeat. This creates a fast trill that sounds unlike anything you could play at that speed using other techniques.

The challenge is to make sure you can remove your fretting hand finger quickly enough to be replaced by the tapping finger. It looks a little crazy on the TAB, so listen to the audio to hear how it is supposed to sound.

Example 3c:

Moving on to a more advanced phrase, this A Minor lick uses two fingers on the tapping hand.

The tapping hand plays the tapped note in a hammer style, similar to playing the keyboard. There are no pull-offs between the tapping hand fingers.

Be aware of controlling the extraneous string noise that can creep in when pulling off to the open G string. The best way I have found to reduce unwanted noise is to mute all the strings with my fretting hand first finger as soon as the 7th fret has been played.

Learn the fretting hand and the tapping hand parts separately, then combine them once memorized

Example 3d:

This lick involves tapping the 12th fret, while the fretting hand ascends in symmetrical octave shapes. The phrase is based on an A Minor Pentatonic scale with an added 9th. All the taps are performed with the middle finger to allow you to hold the pick normally between your thumb and first finger.

The final note can be played in any way that feels comfortable. I often use a hammer-on but other times I will pick it, especially if I want to add vibrato.

Example 3e:

This idea uses a well-known tapping triplet shape and moves it diatonically across the guitar strings. Practice with a metronome to make sure you aren't rushing the string changes and be careful of unwanted noise when changing strings.

Example 3f:

This E Minor phrase is based on the playing of Greg Howe, who uses this kind of tapping mechanic to play arpeggio inversions. Here, I have modified it to use the minor pentatonic scale.

You will need to practice this slowly and memorize the fingering for both hands carefully, as this lick sounds best when played at high speeds. There's a lot going on, so feel free to split the line and just use segments of it in your playing. You do not need to play the whole thing at once and I will often use just the first bar.

Example 3g:

This next phrase is an extension of Example 3g and repeats part of it to create an even more angular sequence. If you have memorized Example 3g it will not be too difficult to master this variation.

As with Example 3g, you don't have to play the whole thing. Split it up and isolate your favourite segments.

Example 3h:

The following E Minor lick is a fluid way to play two complete octaves of the minor pentatonic scale. The hardest part is the hammer-on on the third string, just after the string skip. This note needs to be played with a first finger "hammer-on from nowhere" i.e. without any picking to jumpstart the sound. Make sure you practice this phrase slowly, especially the string skip. Hammer hard!

Example 3i:

This next example is based on the E Minor Pentatonic scale and sounds quite impressive when played up to speed. However, it isn't that challenging to play. Pay attention to keeping the rhythm in tight 1/16th notes and avoid extraneous string noise when changing strings.

Example 3j:

Here's a cool, single-string lick that combines tapping with some wide stretches to create a barrage of notes from the E Minor Pentatonic scale. Even better, there are no string changes to make things challenging.

I have noticed that players often have trouble timing the pull-off between the third and fourth fingers. The best way to fix this is to use a metronome and play two notes per beat. This way, it will be obvious if you are playing the rhythm correctly or not.

Pay attention to the timing, and if you feel any pain when performing the wide stretches stop and give your fingers a break.

Example 3k:

Here's a cool E Minor Pentatonic phrase which is an excellent way to finish a solo, provided you can pull it off convincingly. All the taps are at the 17th fret and the fretting hand is based on the common pentatonic box, so the fingering should not be a problem.

Once you have memorized the shape on the first string, you will be able to breeze through this lick, as the pattern is similar on each string.

Example 3l:

This idea is influenced by Dave Celentano. It is based on the A Minor Pentatonic scale and uses two fingers of the tapping hand to outline an A Minor triad on the 17th fret, while the fretting hand outlines the same A Minor triad in its previous position on the 12th fret. This creates a sound that is reminiscent of a harp.

Several things require your attention here: make sure the timing of the tapping and pull-offs is rhythmically even. Muting will probably be challenging too, as there are a lot of string changes to contend with.

Example 3m:

This A Minor Pentatonic lick uses the edge of the pick to tap and is based around the same chord shapes used in the previous example. The pick taps create a fast, trill-like effect that moves across the top three strings in an energetic way. Mute the strings with your fretting hand throughout.

Listen to the audio file to get a clear idea of how this lick should sound. Pick tapping is a unique approach that offers a new timbre to your arsenal of sounds.

Example 3n:

There's more pick-tapping in this idea influenced by Jake E. Lee. It is based on the A Minor Pentatonic scale and is played on the third string, with the pick edge continuously tapping the 12th fret. This is a great way to move from the 12th fret all the way down to the 2nd fret.

Example 3o:

The following lick is one of my favourite multi-finger tapping patterns. It is based on the A Minor Pentatonic scale and is an extension of the idea presented in Example 3d. However, now we will add an extra note on the first string and tap it with the third finger.

There is no easy way to mute the strings due to the position of both hands. You need to be careful with the first finger pull-off, so it does not hit any other strings. I use my fretting hand first finger to mute all the strings as soon as the note on the 7th fret has been played and I am ready to start tapping.

If you find the tapping part challenging, isolate the tapping notes on the top three strings and practice them separately while muting the strings with the fretting hand first finger. This will help you progress faster than trying to incorporate everything at once.

Learn the parts of the fretting and tapping hands separately before combining them.

Example 3p:

Our final lick for this chapter takes tapping to the next level and uses all four fingers of the tapping hand. The fretting hand is used only for muting.

This is the most difficult lick in this chapter and will give your tapping fingers a good workout. Have fun with it and make sure you stop and take a break if you feel any pain.

The most difficult part of the lick is the accuracy needed to tap the high B note on the 19th fret with the fourth finger, and will probably take some time to master. Make sure you keep your nails short, otherwise they will definitely get in the way!

Example 3q:

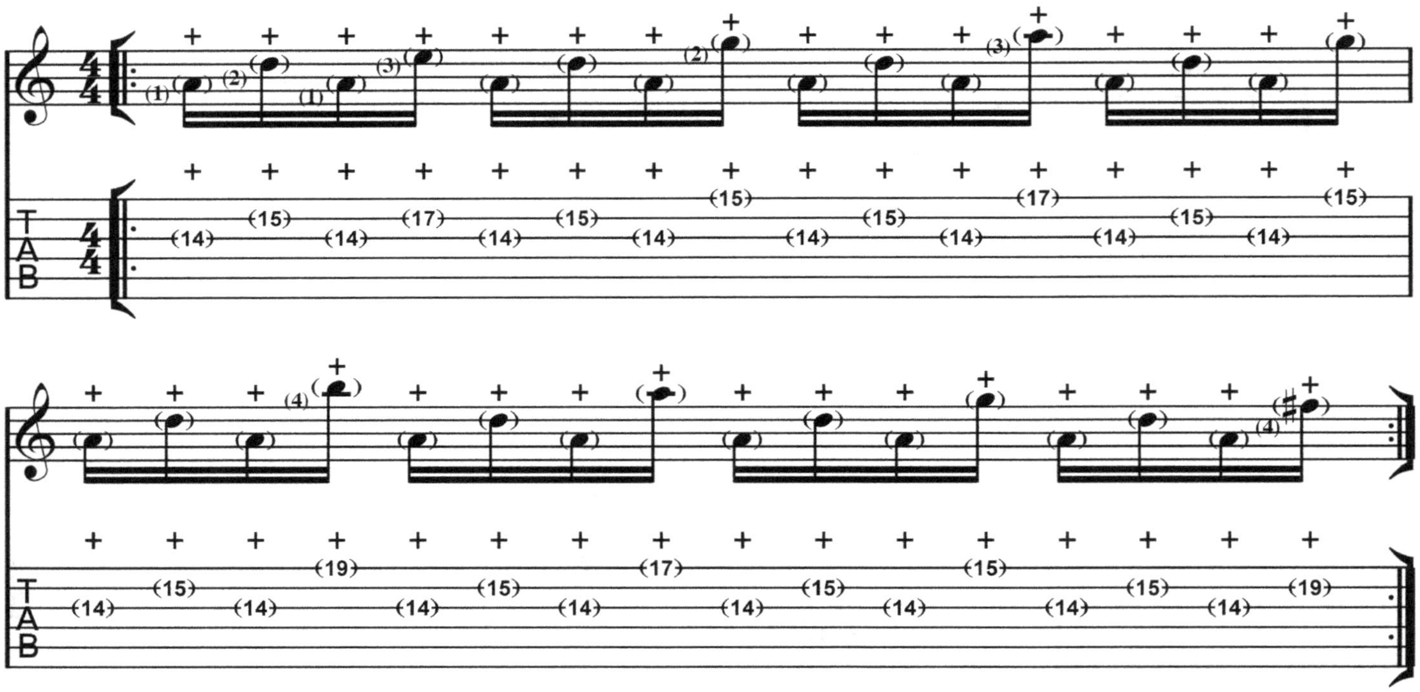

Chapter Four: Hybrid Picking

By using a combination of the pick and picking hand fingers, playing licks that require string skips becomes much easier. Hybrid picking has always been a part of country guitar playing, but it is only in the last 25 years that its use has become a staple of rock. I was taught this technique by Australian rock/fusion virtuoso Brett Garsed, during our lessons in the late '90s, and it has been a major part of my playing ever since.

In hybrid picking, the pick is gripped between the thumb and first finger, while the remaining fingers are used for plucking strings. Mostly, the second and third fingers are used, and they are referred to in the notation using the Spanish classical naming system:

m = medio (middle/second finger)

a = anular (ring/third finger)

In the examples that follow, the notation will indicate which notes are picked and which are plucked with the fingers.

If you are new to this technique, practice it slowly and begin by picking notes across three adjacent strings. You'll play one downward pick stroke, followed by two upstrokes executed with the fingers. Take some time to commit the mechanics of the movement to muscle memory.

Once you become accustomed to the picking pattern, there are two further things to consider. First, pay attention to the dynamics of each string. Producing a consistent volume might prove difficult at first, as not all your picking hand fingers will have the same strength and independence, but this is a goal to aim for.

The second thing to look out for is unwanted string noise. When hybrid picking, you can't use your fingers for muting and noise can become a problem, especially when using distortion. To mitigate this, mute with your fretting hand by using careful finger placement.

Our first example uses the A Minor Pentatonic scale and rearranges it one note per string while moving horizontally down the fretboard. This lick is a great introduction to hybrid picking as it uses a repeated pattern with no rhythmic variation.

The picking pattern is: third finger, second finger, then pick, repeated throughout the lick.

Example 4a:

The second example is probably the hybrid picking pattern I use the most. Once you get the mechanics down it can be played at a decent speed.

The patterns are based on intervals of 4ths and 5ths in A Minor Pentatonic.

There are a couple of technical things to pay attention to. Try not move your picking hand wrist too much. This time the picking pattern is one commonly found in country guitar. If you normally use a heavy attack with your guitar pick, it will probably be necessary to moderate the volume of your picking to match the plucked strings.

Keep your fretting hand in the 12th position and your thumb behind the neck.

Example 4b:

Let's take things up a notch with this elaboration of the pattern used above. It uses the pick and fingers in combination to achieve wide stretches and a series of melodic leaps.

The fretting hand is positioned in the 12th-17th fret area and there are two different vertical shapes used. The whole lick is basically one pattern of eight notes that repeats diatonically on adjacent string groups. Pay attention to the fingering in the notation, otherwise you might struggle to play this cleanly.

As with the previous examples, all the picked notes are played with downstrokes followed by plucked notes with the second and/or third fingers.

Example 4c:

This lick uses a combination of the pick and second finger to play a series of octaves in the A Minor Pentatonic scale. This is another good example of how using hybrid picking makes phrases that would require difficult pick jumps much easier.

Use a fairly light attack with the picked notes to keep the volume as consistent as possible.

Example 4d:

This phrase is a variation of the pattern above, this time in consecutive fifths instead of octaves. Even though this version is slightly easier, both licks add an angular sound to the A Minor Pentatonic scale.

The fast interplay between the pick and finger is a technique often found in country guitar playing. Use a fairly light attack on the picked notes to keep the dynamics as consistent as possible.

Example 4e:

Using a picking hand finger to play a repeating pedal tone is an excellent way to use hybrid picking as a melodic device. This lick combines the A Minor Pentatonic scale (with an added 9th) and a repeating C note to create this characteristic pedal point.

Example 4f:

This A Minor pedal point lick uses lot more repetition.

Using a different finger to play each string makes it easier to play at high speed. All the notes on the third string are played with the pick. Notes on the second/first strings are played with the second/third fingers respectively.

Feel free to use the pattern to come up with your own variations.

Example 4g:

The next example is based on an eight-note sequence which repeats using different arpeggio shapes in the A Minor Pentatonic scale. This is an interesting lick, more reminiscent of a keyboard than guitar, and hybrid picking makes it possible to execute it with similar fluidity.

The basic pattern is eight notes long before the position shift, so memorize the phrase in groups of eight.

Example 4h:

Hybrid picking excels when notes are arranged one note per string. In the following phrase, a series of suspended triads and power chord inversions are played across four strings to take full advantage of this characteristic guitar technique.

This repeating eight-note A Minor Pentatonic phrase is inspired by John Petrucci. Follow the fingering in the notation closely.

Example 4i:

This idea is heavily influenced by Brett Garsed. Brett was one of the first guitar players to effortlessly blend hybrid picking with legato in a rock context. Pay attention to both the fingering and the picking, as there are some tricky parts, especially on the 3rd beat of the first bar.

Example 4j:

This E Minor Pentatonic lick is arranged one note per string over three string groups. The pattern is similar to the one used in Example 4a, but here we have more vertical movement across the strings. Keep your picking light to create a uniform dynamic.

Example 4k:

The final phrase in this chapter is built around the A Minor Pentatonic scale played in wide intervals. Such intervallic leaps aren't often associated with electric guitar, as they are quite difficult to play at a fast tempo, but become much more manageable using a hybrid approach. This lick is influenced by the playing of studio legend, Carl Verheyen (look out for a book from him coming soon from Fundamental Changes!)

Example 4l:

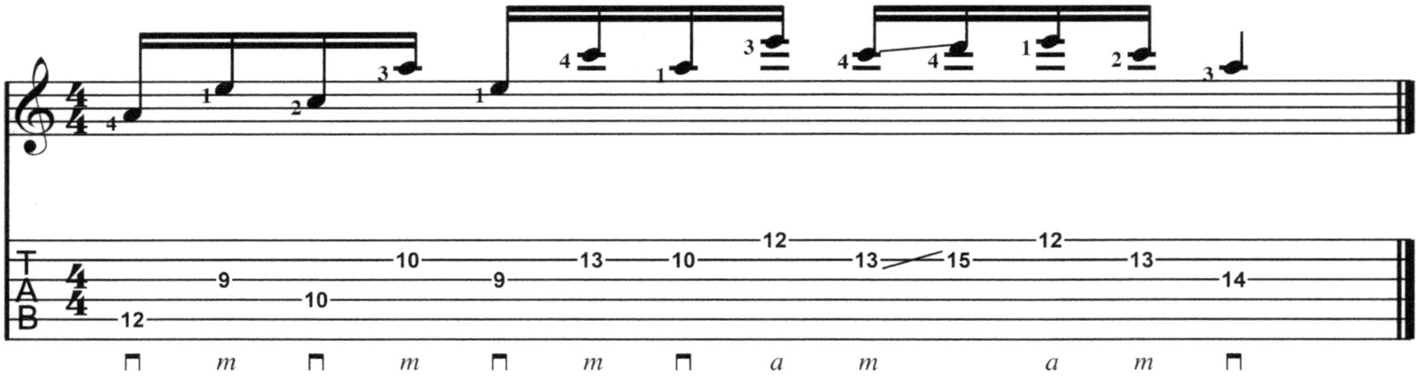

Chapter Five: Wide Stretches

Playing wide stretches is one of the most exciting contemporary techniques for the electric guitar. It's a challenging technique that calls for careful fretting hand positioning, but it's well worth the effort, as it opens up a whole world of sounds. I classify a wide stretch as one that spans more than two tones between the first finger and the fourth finger of the fretting hand.

If you find the stretches too challenging in any of the lines that follow, try moving the whole line higher up the neck so the fret distances are smaller.

We'll begin with an impressive phrase that combines legato with wide stretches and a little bit of sweeping. It's played high up the neck, so the stretch shouldn't be a problem for most players, provided you keep the fretting hand fingers straight and parallel to the frets. Keep your thumb behind the neck, not on top of it.

Example 5a:

The second phrase re-rearranges the E Minor Pentatonic scale to fit a three-note-per-string alternate picking approach. This is an interesting idea, as this kind of fast-picked sequencing isn't normally associated with the pentatonic scale. The stretches are not too difficult provided you keep a good fretting hand position, but work at getting the fast alternate picking consistently accurate.

Example 5b:

Here's a cool E Minor Pentatonic phrase influenced by Kee Marcello. The idea is to play the scale in ascending quintuplets using a repeating pattern of two notes on the lower string followed by three notes on the higher string. The use of quintuplets adds some unpredictability to the line.

Example 5c:

This challenging Rusty Cooley inspired phrase uses the E Minor Pentatonic scale with an added 9th and arranges it in a four-note-per-string pattern. The stretch on the first string is three-and-a-half whole steps and on the second string it is four! Realistically, this is the largest stretch you would ever need to use, so take care you do not injure your wrist/fingers.

Practice each string shape separately before putting them together. Feel free to play extra repetitions on each string if it feels easier.

If you are new to these wide stretches, don't dive straight into this example. Start by learning a few of the easier licks before tackling this one. That said, once you have it under your fingers, this is one of the most impressive licks you'll ever learn.

Example 5d:

This E Minor Pentatonic example uses a combination of legato, wide stretches and repeated notes to create a modern effect. Take your time when memorizing this line, as it can be a little tricky to get the picking and legato combination right. The pattern is 12 notes long, and you can repeat it as many times as you like.

Listen to the audio file for extra help; licks with repeated notes tend to make much more sense when you listen to them played up to speed.

Example 5e:

This next E Minor lick is influenced by the playing of George Lynch (Dokken) and combines legato and wide stretches with sweeping to facilitate string changes. The repeating notes between the first and second string gives this phrase an unexpected twist, which makes it sound quite unusual.

Example 5f:

This E Minor Pentatonic lick uses legato and wide stretches to create a long, flowing descending line. The pattern is a popular sextuplet legato idea, but one that is rarely used in a pentatonic setting, as it requires wider stretches to incorporate the notes. Here I've arranged the patterns so that the fingerings are symmetrical and easier to perform.

Example 5g:

This E Minor Pentatonic lick spans more than two full octaves and uses a symmetrical fingering, with the first, second and fourth fingers for most of the lick, to make the stretches a little easier.

It sounds impressive at full speed – almost like a car motor revving higher and higher!

Aim for a consistent volume when changing strings and keep an even rhythm between every note. Record your playing with a metronome. This will immediately help you to spot any rhythmic inconsistencies.

As a final performance point, pay attention to the picking directions. The first note is a downstroke but every other picked note is an upstroke.

Example 5h:

Here is an imaginative combination of legato and wide stretches on adjacent strings.

The first string outlines an E Minor triad and the second string a B Minor triad. The combination of the two triads creates an E Minor Pentatonic scale with an added 9th, but the way it is performed sounds exciting and fresh.

I play just one pick stroke every two beats, on the string change from the second to first string. All the other notes are played legato.

The legato pattern isn't too difficult, but the stretches can be challenging, so take a break if you feel any pain in your wrist or fingers. To minimize the risk, keep your thumb straight behind the neck and your fretting fingers parallel to the frets throughout the whole lick.

Example 5i:

This descending sextuplet line is based on the E Minor Pentatonic scale and uses a combination of legato and wide stretching. You can hear similar patterns in the playing of Kee Marcello, Joe Satriani and Eric Johnson.

Only the first note is picked – all the rest are achieved with either hammer-ons or pull-offs.

Example 5j:

This phrase is one of my favourites since it combines legato, wide stretches and some fluid slides to create a particularly exciting approach.

If you have managed to play the other licks in this chapter, the legato and wide stretching shouldn't be too difficult, but the slides will take some work to perform properly. It can be difficult to play the slides in time at full tempo, as they are performed both sliding *towards* the target note *and* out of it. This requires extreme accuracy which might take time to develop. Listen to the audio to hear this approach.

Practice this lick with a metronome and don't get discouraged if it takes time to speed up those pesky slides.

Example 5k:

Our final wide stretching lick is an idea based on descending E Minor Pentatonic quintuplets. Similar sounding phrases are often used by Eric Johnson and John Petrucci.

The notes are arranged in two adjacent positions to get the most out of the melodic pattern. It is built around a two-string shape, with three notes on the higher string and two on the lower string.

Example 5l:

Chapter Six: String Skipping

Skipping strings is another way in which we can access much larger intervals in our solos, which can help us to avoid clichéd licks and sound less obviously guitar-like. They are usually played with either alternate or hybrid picking.

This first string skipping phrase is built around the A Minor Pentatonic scale with an added 9th. The combination of repeating notes on the fourth string, with an ascending legato idea, creates a particularly unique approach.

I often add some palm muting to the fourth string to make the notes pop out a little more, and accentuate the difference in tone between the first part of each sextuplet and the second.

Example 6a:

This A Minor idea takes a popular descending triplet pattern and rearranges it to use several string skips. The use of several octave intervals creates a more angular sound. I use hybrid picking to play the string skips, but you can also try alternate picking if you prefer.

Example 6b:

Here is another exciting lick that alternates between fifth and octaves intervals, while staying firmly in A Minor Pentatonic. I suggest you use hybrid picking here – it will make the string skips much easier

Example 6c:

Now let's use string skipping to create a long flowing melody that spans three full octaves of the A Minor Pentatonic scale. The combination of picking, legato and hybrid picking creates a fluid, almost liquid sound.

Pay attention to any extraneous string noise that might creep in, especially when changing positions. To minimize this noise, slightly flatten your first finger, so that it lightly touches the higher strings and stops them ringing.

Example 6d:

The following E Minor lick is technically advanced and uses wide stretches combined with string skipping and legato. If you find the stretches too difficult, move the whole lick higher up the neck to reduce the distance you need to stretch.

Memorize the picking directions and fingering carefully. The first note is a downstroke and is followed by two upstrokes then another downstroke before the pattern repeats.

Example 6e:

The following A Minor lick combines string skips, legato and wide stretches to create a long line of descending sextuplets. Practice this with a metronome as it's easy to rush the pull-offs. The aim is to play a smooth line with even rhythms and controlled dynamics.

If you find yourself rushing the pull-offs, learn the whole phrase as 1/16th notes instead of triplets, as this will help even out any inconsistencies.

Example 6f:

This example is an elaborate variation of the previous idea. It uses a quintuplet pattern that descends all the way down to the sixth string. The wide stretches make this technically challenging, especially on the low strings. Only pick the first note on each string; the rest are played legato.

Example 6g:

Here is one of my favourite technical ideas, which I have used different variations of for almost 20 years.

It is based on the E Minor Pentatonic scale and combines legato, string skips, wide stretches *and* tapping! You'll need to invest some time to learn it, with careful memorization and slow practice. Remember, always stop playing and take a break if you feel any pain in your wrist or fingers.

The most challenging part is the stretch. Keep your hand straight and your thumb behind the neck otherwise you will not be able to reach.

All the notes are legato except the first on each string when ascending. In the first bar, use the underside of your first finger to mute any unplayed strings.

The taps are played with the middle finger, which allows you to hold the pick between your thumb and first finger as normal.

Example 6h:

This E Minor lick has repeating notes on the fourth string to create a strong melodic structure. The string skips makes it sounds as if the guitar is a muscle car revving the gas!

Provided you can play the stretch without too much trouble, it shouldn't be difficult to master this, even at a higher tempo, as the pattern is quite predictable.

Despite it looking like a long phrase, the notes on the fourth string are repeated several times so it won't be too difficult to learn.

Example 6i:

This Carl Verheyen inspired phrase is another favourite of mine and is based around the A Minor Pentatonic scale. It uses the notes of an Am7 arpeggio played at the 12th position but arranged in various octaves.

Example 6j:

The next A Minor Pentatonic idea uses a well-known pattern of descending triplets, arranged to include some wide intervallic leaps created with string skips. You will probably be familiar with the traditional triplet pattern but nailing the string skips might take a little time.

Use hybrid picking for this idea, alternating between third finger plucks and pick downstrokes, which will make it much easier to jump across the strings.

Example 6k:

Chapter Seven: Combining Approaches

We have now covered several different techniques to expand the sonic range of the traditional pentatonic sound. The next logical step is to combine these techniques in ways that will amplify their individual characteristics to create an even more interesting palette.

The first phrase is based on E Minor Pentatonic and combines legato with wide stretches and tapping to create four-note-per-string patterns.

Use the first, second, and fourth fingers to play the stretches on both strings, to help make the position shifts easier.

All taps are performed with the middle finger, while holding the pick between thumb and first finger, even though the pick is not used in the lick.

Example 7a:

The next E Minor Pentatonic idea combines wide stretches with string skipping and tapping to create a challenging lick. Pay attention to your muting, as string skipping tends to create a fair amount of extraneous string noise.

The phrase is based on a ten-note pattern that repeats and descends on different strings. Once you've learned the notes on the first string, the contour of the others is identical. When jumping from the first string to the third, release the pressure on the final note of the first string to stop the string from ringing.

The taps only occur on the 14th and 15th frets, which makes things a little easier. In the fretting hand, the first finger always plays the 7th fret and the fourth finger plays the 12th, to frame the lick nicely and make both the memorization and performance less daunting

Example 7b:

Previously, we've played four-note-per-string ideas but now let's extend that to five notes per string.

To execute this lick, four notes need to be performed with a challenging wide stretch of the fretting hand before tapping on the 24th fret.

Try using the edge of the pick to tap, as it is quite difficult to use a finger so high up the neck.

Example 7c:

This A Minor Pentatonic pattern is based on the playing of Michael Romeo (Symphony X).

There are two technical challenges here:

The first is the "hammer-on from nowhere", where you fret a note using the first finger *without* picking. The idea is to bring your finger down from nowhere with enough force to sound the pitch cleanly.

The second challenge is the high level of muting required. Use the underside of the first finger on the fretting hand to mute the higher strings. Keep your first finger slightly flat across the fretboard, so that it lightly touches the second and first string to stop them ringing.

Pay attention to the fingering. You will see that the first finger always plays the 12th fret and the little finger always plays the 17th.

Experiment by using the edge of the pick for the taps since it will give additional separation to the notes.

Example 7d:

The next idea combines taps with string skips to descend the A Minor Pentatonic scale in octaves. The same four-note sequence is played one octave lower each time. This lick sounds impressive but isn't too difficult once you get used to the position changes.

Example 7e:

The A Minor lick below works as a quick-and-dirty ending to a solo and combines tapping, string skipping and wide stretches.

Notice that the first finger always plays the 12th fret and the fourth finger always plays the 17th. This helps frame the position of the lick and makes it easier to remember.

Example 7f:

Now it's time to expand our tapping skills!

This lick uses two picking hand fingers to tap notes and facilitates playing all five notes of the E Minor Pentatonic scale on a single string.

The pattern is eight notes long then repeats, so it is not difficult to learn – just make sure you use strict 1/16th notes throughout. Getting the first three notes in time will take some getting used to, but once you have them down, you'll have a new weapon in your tapping arsenal.

I have found that using both the second and third finger is a great step for those wishing to expand their playing beyond the usual single-finger tapping patterns. It extends the reach of your playing without necessitating a major change in technique.

The lick starts with the second finger of the picking hand tapping the 17th fret before the third finger taps the 19th. This is followed by a pull-off back to the 17th. You can pull off either towards the floor or up towards the palm of the hand. I tend to use the former method when playing on the first string but the latter if I am tapping on inside strings.

Example 7g:

This A Minor Pentatonic lick is a combination of wide stretches, string skips and taps.

The intense stretch on the first string will be difficult to execute properly for most people with regular sized hands. If you are having trouble, play the phrase in a higher position. For example, try moving it three steps higher and play it using the C Minor Pentatonic scale. Practice it slowly and make sure you stop if you feel any wrist pain.

All taps are played with the middle finger on the 12th fret.

The first note of the lick is tapped and gives you time to prepare your fretting hand for the pull-offs. When skipping to the third string, keep your fretting hand first finger flat so that it mutes the second string.

The final note is a hammer-on from nowhere. Aim to execute this as cleanly as possible.

Example 7h:

Here's an extreme lick based on the E Minor Pentatonic scale that blurs the line between electric guitar and keyboards. Don't expect to master this one quickly, as it will probably take a period of study, even for an advanced player. Once you can play it at speed, however, the work will totally be worth it.

Follow the fingering suggestions closely as they are optimized to help you get the lick up to speed. The notes on the fourth string are played legato and repeated as an ostinato figure, with string skipping patterns interspersed between the repetitions.

Example 7i:

This E Minor Pentatonic lick combines wide stretches with tapping on the 16th and 17th frets. Play the first note of the lick with a strong hammer-on-from-nowhere to get things rolling. The main pattern is repeated diatonically on each descending string.

Even though the pick is not used, I suggest you play this lick holding it as you normally would. This is a good habit to build, as it means you can always transition smoothly from tapping to picking in a solo.

Example 7j:

Pattern repetition is a common characteristic of rock guitar soloing and the next line uses this approach in an exciting way. It combines wide stretches with tapping and uses shapes that masterfully outline the E Minor Pentatonic scale. Even though this phrase sounds great, it is not difficult to play provided the timing is followed carefully.

Example 7k:

This is my absolute favourite pentatonic combination lick and spans more than two octaves of the A Minor Pentatonic scale with a combination of sweeps, wide stretches, string skips and taps. It's based around an Am7 arpeggio played at the 12th fret.

One challenge in its execution is on the final beat, where you need to move from tapping to sweeping very quickly, which demands good accuracy.

Start by picking close to the neck. Picking closer to the 20th fret will make it much easier to transition from picking to tapping. Keep in mind that the string skip from the first string to the third string is a hammer-on from nowhere.

Example 7l:

The following repeating E Minor lick combines wide stretches, string skipping and tapping. Don't worry too much about the 7/4 time signature, just practice it in regular 1/16th notes and it will make sense as you gain speed.

Example 7m:

Chapter Eight: Hi-Tech Blues Scale Licks

The next step in our hi-tech journey is to expand the pentatonic scale by adding the flat fifth "blue note" to invigorate its melodic qualities.

In this section, we will examine several phrases that use the blues scale in combination with the extended techniques we have studied in the previous chapters.

The first lick is based on the E Blues scale and uses a combination of legato and hybrid picking. It is not technically challenging but sounds good when you get it up to speed. The repetition of the same five notes on the third string creates a strong melodic structure that makes this phrase memorable.

Example 8a:

The next idea is based on the A Blues scale and uses a combination of sweeps and legato. While this is not a particularly challenging lick from a technical point of view, it sounds great up to tempo as it creates a seamless volley of notes.

Try to play the sweep lightly to keep the pick noise as low as possible.

Example 8b:

Based on the playing of fusion maestro Greg Howe, this A Minor Pentatonic lick uses a barring technique with the third finger to help reach a high speed. All the notes on the second string are repeated with only the highest note on the first string changing pitch on each repetition. This is an easy phrase to play, but creates a dynamic effect.

Both the picked notes are played with a single up-sweep. Play it lightly to keep the pick noise as low as possible.

The third finger barres the top two strings and stays there for three notes without moving. Follow the picking directions carefully and this will make sense as soon as you memorize the phrase.

Example 8c:

This A Blues phrase is based on the playing of Frank Gambale and borrows a note from the A Dorian mode to keep the sweep shape consistent across the strings.

Follow the fingering carefully. Each finger takes care of one fret. All the notes on the 5th fret are played by the first finger, notes on the 7th by the third finger, and notes on the 8th by the fourth finger. Minimize string noise by using a rolling barre.

The most challenging part of this lick is rolling the fourth finger – a move many guitar players are not familiar with – so practice the movement slowly to lock it into muscle memory.

Example 8d:

The next phrase is a natural expansion of an idea we saw way back in Chapter One (Example 1l). This example adds the blues note to that pattern to extend it and make it more interesting.

Make sure you target the 17th and 18th frets carefully. They are easy to miss, as they are both played with the fourth finger.

The phrase starts with an upstroke and a trill on the first string. This is followed by three alternate picked notes on the second string.

Example 8e:

Adding the blues note makes it easier to use three-note-per-string patterns in your playing, an idea that is demonstrated in next two examples. Even though both examples use the same sequence, the first is a little trickier due to the wide stretch on the first string.

Here you'll play five notes per beat using only the first, third, and fourth fingers. I have opted to pick the first note on each string to create a stronger rhythmic accent. Focus on the third finger as it remains on the 15th fret during the whole lick.

Example 8f:

This is one of my go-to licks when I want a fluid, repeating blues sound. I tend to use upstrokes to cross the strings, to help my muting and minimize any extraneous string noise.

Example 8g:

Virtuoso guitarist Steve Vai is the inspiration behind the following E Blues scale line. Played on the first string with a combination of legato and tapping, it sounds intense due to its unique combination of repeated notes and speedy triplet taps.

The fourth note is the same as the third, but played with the tapping finger to create a short, fast trill. This is an excellent idea to spice up your usual approach and is fairly easy to play.

The main challenge is to get your fretting hand ring finger out of the way after it has played its note, so that it can be replaced by the tapping finger. It looks a little strange in the notation, so listen to the audio example to hear how it's supposed to sound.

Example 8h:

This A Blues lick is influenced by George Lynch (Dokken, Lynch Mob), who often uses the blues scale in exciting, unexpected ways.

Here, taps are used to create repeating trills that emphasize the blues note. You can use your third finger for the tapping, or the side of your guitar pick. If you opt for the latter, the sound will be brighter and more aggressive.

I prefer using the pick for the tap as it creates a brighter tone and it's easier to play double-taps. This lick looks difficult on paper, but with the exception of the first two beats, it's all built from the same sequence, with the tapped note moving diatonically up the first string.

This is one of those phrases that looks (and sounds) scary, but once memorized it's not too difficult to play, even at a high speed. Hearing the audio example will help you, so make sure you check it out.

Example 8i:

Our final A Blues phrase is a variation of Example 8e and uses the same picking pattern. The combination of several picked notes with legato creates an exciting energy as the two techniques contrast sharply.

Example 8j:

Conclusion

Well, there you have it. I hope you've enjoyed playing these ideas as much as I've enjoyed writing them. My goal has been to offer you an exciting collection of ideas that use the pentatonic scale in progressively more original ways.

Not all the phrases included will appeal to everyone, so pick and choose the ones you like according to your taste and ability. I encourage you to experiment with all the different techniques used, but pay attention to what your hands are telling you. If you feel any pain when practising these licks, especially the wide stretches, stop playing immediately, take a break and try again later when you have adequately recovered. Avoiding injury is an important part of continuously improving your guitar playing skills.

I hope you found this book exciting, challenging, and musically rewarding. Good luck and see you next time!

Ioannis

Acknowledgements

I would like to thank all those who helped in the writing and editing of this book. Many thanks to Joseph Alexander for giving me the opportunity to present my work in this format.

Most importantly, my parents, Konstantinos and Efthalia Anastassakis, for their unwavering help and encouragement (as well as the occasional, much-needed reality check).

My good friends and guitar students Theodore Kalantzakos, Antonis Rafeletos, Jim Nassios, Nick Tasioulas, Nikos Delis and Alex Mitsou, for their invaluable help in proof-reading the original texts and scores and catching (hopefully most) of my writing mistakes.

Finally, I want to thank my good friend Bob Katsionis, for his assistance with the recording and mastering process of the audio for this book.

Special thanks to all my guitar teachers who openly shared their knowledge with me, so I can now share these ideas with you in this book.

About the Author

Born on the Greek island of Crete, Ioannis Anastassakis studied at the distinguished Musicians Institute (GIT), where he stayed on as a tutor, after graduating in the top 1% of his class. He continued his graduate studies, completing an MA in Guitar Performance, graduating Magna cum Laude.

The list of teachers Ioannis has studied with reads like a who's who of contemporary electric guitar legends: Steve Vai, Vinnie Moore, Kiko Loureiro, Marty Friedman, John Petrucci, Frank Gambale, Paul Gilbert, Brett Garsed and Scott Henderson.

Ioannis has performed over 400 solo guitar recitals in Europe and the US, and has been a guest lecturer at several American colleges and universities. In addition, he has won classical and flamenco guitar competitions, has been featured 12 times on American TV, and was the first guitarist ever to present a solo guitar recital at the Greek National Opera House. He has released four instrumental guitar CDs, in the genres of flamenco and rock/fusion, and has authored several guitar instructional books/DVDs.

Ioannis is sponsored by Ibanez electric guitars (6-string), Schecter electric guitars (7-string), Roland guitar effects, EMG active pickups, Elixir instrument cables, LaBella flamenco guitar strings, T-Rex effects pedals, Visual Sound effects pedals, Hercules stands, Graphtech custom guitar parts, Snapjack jacks and George-L studio cables.

Ioannis taught Guitar and Music Business at the American College of Greece for 10 years. In 2011, he founded the Elite Guitar Coaching Academy, an online guitar academy that helps guitar players from around the world to reach their full playing potential. You can check out the academy at **www.eliteguitarcoaching.com**

For up to date information about Ioannis, visit his official website: **www.ioannis.org**

www.ingramcontent.com/pod-product-compliance
Lightning Source LLC
Chambersburg PA
CBHW081438090426
42740CB00017B/3356